Shacklette Elementary
FRC Presents

Trailblazers Pathways to Success

BK
ROYSTON
Publishing

BK Royston Publishing
P. O. Box 4321
Jeffersonville, IN 47131
502-802-5385
http://www.bkroystonpublishing.com
bkroystonpublishing@gmail.com

Imagine ME LLC
P.O. Box 16583
Louisville, Kentucky 40256
(502) 802-5962
Imaginemerising@gmail.com

Cover Design: Elite Book Covers

ISBN-13: 978-1-955063-14-2

Printed in the United States of America

Dedication

This work is dedicated to every child who dreams of becoming. It is dedicated to every child who is brave enough to imagine better. It is dedicated to every child who embraces inspiration. And to every adult who speaks greatness over the life of a child knowing they are creating possibilities for the child to dream, imagine, and rise in peace to inspire others.

These are the true Trailblazers!

Imagine ME, LLC

Acknowledgements

"If there's a book that you want to read, but it hasn't been written yet, then you must write it."
--Toni Morrison

Nothing grants more satisfaction than the realization of my daily life making a positive difference in the lives of others.

Greater satisfaction can only come from acknowledging the tremendous impact of these same lives upon my service and daily bread.

I am elated to be a promoter of young people as they advance through their journey and experience all that life promises to teach.

The Shacklette Elementary Family Resource Center and the Shacklette Elementary School Administration wishes to extend our most sincere gratitude to all who collaborated to make this project a reality for our students. Thank you to our Principal, Mr. Kevin Garner for taking a leap of faith and graciously supporting this endeavor. Thank you to each parent and family member who supported their student in becoming a published author! Your dedication to the process was pivotal and has paid off in ways yet to be seen. I want to extend deep gratitude to the dynamic collaborative partnership of Dr. Julia

Royston of BK Royston Publishing and to Imagine ME, LLC for the creative and passionate way in which you enjoy sharing the writing process with children. Your professional investment and expertise made this process a gift to all.

Last, but certainly not least in any way; Thank you to each student who accepted the challenge to blaze a new trail and share their legacy with the world. That which is written shall never be forgotten.

Students remember to be proud of who you are, where you come from, and where you plan to go! You can do whatever you set your mind to, so choose your thoughts carefully as your deeds are certain to follow.

All the best,

Ms. Angela Eddings, Coordinator

Shacklette Elementary School

Family Resource Center

Table of Contents

FOREWORD

"Inspire greatness in others and it will be easier to inspire greatness in you."

Anonymous

<u>Destined for Greatness.</u>

Hello, my name is Bryce C. Royles and I am 12 years old in the 6th grade. I enjoy acting, drawing, writing, and cooking. Ever since I was little, I knew I was meant for something great and as I grew older,

I thought more and more about my future and the things I wanted to do. I want to use my talents to become an actor and a singer. Although I knew this by the age of seven, I have grown to love the arts even more. So much so that it has now expanded to writing and drawing. My dad was a musician, my mom has studied writing since she was a teenager, and my stepdad is a doctor. Each of my parents have always had something unique and amazing about them. They have a talent, a skill; something great that became a part of who I am. Thanks to my dad, I have musical talent which I grow every day. Thanks to my mom, I have learned to express my voice through writing. And thanks to my stepfather, I have the desire to help people. My parents taught me how to grow in my ability and use it for the good of others. Like many amazing artists, I can use my talent to follow my dreams and inspire others to do the same. I can inspire people to do good by doing good myself.

When I become a star, I want to use my platform to raise money for charity and many great causes. I will help the homeless, the less fortunate, and the underprivileged. I will create change to lessen the impact of racism, sexism, and many other problems that plague our world. I will do amazing things to help improve and strengthen this world. I will do things to spread joy and bring happiness. I believe I will make the world better like all the kind and brave people that came before me.

As the amazing trailblazer Rev. Dr. Martin Luther King, Jr. once stated, "If you can't fly then run, if you can't run then walk, if you can't walk then crawl, but whatever you do, you have to keep moving forward!" Keeping that in mind, I know that I will do extraordinary things. I am on an incredible journey

and I will blaze my trail!

I am a Trailblazer destined for

greatness!

Bryce C. Royles

Trailblazers

Julia Bunzy

"Mistakes are proof that you are learning."

Ben Francia

My name is Julia Bunzy, and I am an eleven-year-old student. One of the most fabulous things about me is I ABSOLUTELY LOVE to learn. If you know me then you may know about my newfound love for knitting and crocheting. In November 2020, I learned how to knit. My PE teacher at school shared with me how to knit and I have enjoyed perfecting my craft. Around January 2021, my PE teacher also taught me how to crochet! For my 11th birthday, my

"Grandshamomma" gave me a loom. I really enjoy using my loom to create beautiful things. I guess you can say in addition to being a person who loves to learn, I am also creative and hardworking. I enjoy talking and meeting new people and it excites me to help others and see things in our world become better. I have four older siblings and three younger siblings. As an older sister, I want to make sure I set a good example for my younger siblings.

I believe that my part in this world is to work on making the world a better place for children. I want to make sure children are happy, safe, and healthy. Some of the things that I see in the world today that make it an unsafe place for children is the violence against one another. It seems like someone is always dying from an act of violence against them by someone else. Some of the violence that ends in deaths are unintentional because it is caused by someone trying to defend themselves or their family members. But most of the violence that ends in death is caused by people who just have no respect for the life of another person. They are angry or unhealthy in their mind and it causes them to do things to other people without a valid reason. I believe that fatally abusing someone should have consequences that are greater and stricter than what we see in the world today. It bothers me to know that someone can shoot another person because they just do not like them or cause them to die because of the color of their skin. Racism driven killings are the worst ever. Killing someone for a reason they cannot change, or control is a very evil and intentional act of violence. The government must take this more seriously or things will only continue to get even more dangerous for the entire human race.

Another problem in the world that makes things unsafe and unhealthy for children is the way kids can watch television, misuse technology, and stay inside the house so much. Watching a lot of television is not good for your mind and it is not good for your body. Sitting in front of a game or a device all day does not teach you anything except the negative stuff you see on the screen. Children are no longer playing outside and making new friends. Kids do not play with other kids and when they do, they either fight, argue, or talk about things they should not be talking about. Kids do not know how to be friends with each other anymore. I believe this is because they are always in the house watching television or playing video games. Kids do not talk to each other or play together in games like hopscotch or O.U.T.-OUT. They choose smartphones over learning about the environment by being in it and seeing what happens every day. Kids should be required to play outside, and parents should have to be there to watch and make sure they are playing outside games. Parents should not give children devices that have grown-up apps and social media. All this together makes kids unhealthy both physically and emotionally. I know some kids who say they cannot go one day without their game or their phone. I know kids who are on social media seeing things that are too old for their age. All the ads that pop-up during a search online should be good for kids to see also. I cannot even search a recipe for lemonade online without an ad popping up on my screen trying to sell me a foot massage. It just is not right to force kids to be grown-ups. It can cause them to be too grown before they need to and then when they are grown, they are worn out by life. Then they are not able to enjoy being an adult.

I have so many things I know I can do and become when I am older, but the most important to me is to be happy. And the other is to help change the way the world treats kids. Kids' lives matter because their lives turn into the adults we will be someday. If we are not healthy adults, it is probably because we were not healthy kids. And I, Julia Bunzy, plan on doing my part to at least change it in whatever place I live as an adult. My plan to change up the game in this world is to become a Politician and an Activist that fights for the rights of people to live without fear of violence and to make the world safer, healthier, and happier for kids to live. I learned from my father about laws and amendments that affect us as human beings. I have read some and found out that even though they say one thing, they can be used in a different way. For example, the Fourth Amendment and the Thirteenth Amendment are written to protect only certain people. Those certain people are the people who write them and their friends and family. That carries on for years even after they are no longer alive. This is how we have some of the laws written today. So, my goal is to work on changing the laws to make them better for the safety of everyone, especially kids. I will be a game changer who changes the world by changing the laws!

Some of the things that are legal would become illegal. This starts with children being on social media. Kids would not be able to use social media on their devices unless they are at least 18 years old and have a valid way to prove their age. Parents would not be allowed to let their kids use social media at all. Kids would not be able to have a cell phone until they are a student in middle school and make good grades. The phone would block all apps and must be purchased by an adult for the kids. The adult will have to show identification and agree to follow the laws about kids and cell phones. Social media would only be allowed for people 18 years old and up and accounts would be created with an official adult email. Proof of identity would be required before the account can be approved for use. Kids should not use adult accounts at all. And any adult violating this law will be considered an offender. The adult would be charged and have a consequence of either a large fine or jail time. If any adult keeps breaking this law, they can receive 3 years in jail for each crime.

The final laws I want to create would be laws about children and technology.

Instead of using technology so much, kids would be going outside to play. I would make it mandatory for kids to have outside activity every day of the week for at least two hours per day. During that time, the adult keeping the child will have to supervise the child and make sure they are not using technology but playing actual games with other children. Television for kids would be limited to specific times and kids may only watch Disney Plus or shows that are appropriate for young children. Television station companies will not be allowed to air shows for children that have adult matters in them. They would be restricted to airing television shows for 12 hours or less during the day. Shows aired during the weekday must be educational and shows on the weekends can only be cartoons, movies, or shows for kids. Shows for kids cannot have commercials or ads. This means the television station companies will have special channels for kids and they would be separate from adult channels. The adult channels will be locked and can only be unlocked with a special government-issued code. All technology and screen time will be tracked and reported to an agency that will monitor if people are following the technology laws. If people do not follow the laws, they lose their technology privileges in their household. I believe that if people knew how positive the effects of technology laws were, they would not want to break them.

Becoming the mayor of a struggling city, or even a part of the legislative branch is my trail to blaze. I believe that people will understand the changes to make the world a better place and see them as great changes. There is so much trauma and drama in the world today. Kids are being hurt by violence, taken captive by technology, and led wrong by what they see and hear on social media and television. Someone must take a stand. And I am just fine with that someone being me. Even if no one believes in my political dreams and ideas for safer children, it will not stop me from fighting for these changes. These changes mean safer cities and less trauma. And these two things mean safer, healthier, and happier kids living in this world!

Zieland Anderson

"Everything negative-
pressure, challenges-is all an
opportunity for me to rise."
Kobe Bryant

Hello world, I am Zieland Anderson. I am a ten-year-old rising 6th grade scholar at Shacklette Elementary. As a rule, I am excited about living life every day. When I open my eyes every morning, I am thankful for all the talents and blessings I receive daily due to the hard work and support of my wonderful mother. It is because of her that I love to learn, I am a leader, and have the opportunity to play basketball. Basketball is my favorite sport and I enjoy playing it. I believe I am a good basketball player too! I am also a fan of equality and treating others right. Therefore, seeing the plague of racism in our world and its effects on our daily life is truly something I want to see change. I am a firm believer that everyone can find a way to greatly impact the world in a positive way and make it better for others. And of course, I want to be in the history books and able to make my family proud of my name. I want to be able to combine my passion for social justice with my love for basketball and make changes the world has never seen before.

Combining my love for basketball with my passion for equality will take great leadership and commitment on my part. To be a leader does not always mean you tell people what to do. Sometimes it means guiding others to present the best of themselves through leading by example. I want to be a leader that sets a great example for those following me. One way I can do this is by always giving my best in school and making good grades. I can be a great role model for my peers and younger family members by showing them what hard work looks like. At the same time, I will be benefiting myself because, in the end, the hard work will pay off.

Throughout my career as an elementary, middle, and high school student, I will be working hard. Not only academically, but also by improving in sports and athletic ability. Being a great student and role model, while also working to get better and better at basketball by playing on teams throughout middle and high school could be challenging, but I have learned that nothing good ever comes easy. Only by hard work and perseverance can someone be truly successful. I plan to use that success not only to benefit myself, but also my community and even the whole world.

After high school, I will need a plan to get into a good college. Having those good grades will pay off now, because they are going to look great on my college applications. And, of course, the college I choose to attend will have a basketball team where I can challenge myself even more and improve every day. The only way to improve is to be challenged. College is one of the biggest challenges of all, especially for athletic students who must balance sports and academics. I will also have to develop responsibility because I will be away from home and making decisions every day without depending on my family as much. But I know that there is no challenge I will face that I cannot overcome.

Once I have worked, made the grades and graduated college, I hope to be a first-round draft pick for the National Basketball Association (NBA). This goal of mine will push my limits as an athlete the entire time, but I know I can do it. I will be the best player that I can be. Giving my one-hundred percent effort is something that I will have done all throughout my life up to this point and being drafted is proof of that. There will not be time to slow down now except to enjoy my success and take care of my family!

Being an athlete often means having a lot of money thrown at you at the beginning of your career, but sometimes people fail to manage that money correctly and end up worse than they started off. I understand that managing that money the right way is important to my dreams and a vital part of my plan to make change in the world. In fact, I plan to hire a financial advisor to help me with this plan. My mother and my grandmother say it is a good idea to have money invested in many places. Investments are ways for your money to grow on its own. So, I will put money away for an important project. Meanwhile, I will keep playing basketball nationally, against some great players, and put my skills to the test.

Once enough money has been saved, I plan to open a social justice and racial equality education camp for children and young people.

People always say that children are the future. So, I am going to impact the future by serving children like me. The camp will be remote and will not tolerate hate or disrespect from one group to another. It will teach compassion, respect, self-love, and cultural acceptance to young people in a real way. That does not mean just getting to know each other's names and what their favorite foods are.

That means learning about each other's culture and understanding the different struggles that we all go through.

Then begin to see everyone, no matter their background, as a valuable human being. This camp will bring young people together of all different races and provide experiences that challenge them to learn more about one another through our own research and firsthand account. It will welcome questions and answers for understanding and sharing of our own lives so we can better empathize with one another.

Ending racism is a big project, and one that cannot be solved in one lifetime or by one person. But starting with youthful individuals and raising a generation of acceptance and consideration, this will hopefully be a good start. I want to prove to everyone that no matter what your position is in society, you can make a difference.

I feel if we all come together and treat each other with respect and dignity, the world would be a better place. It is our right to stand up for what we believe, and I plan to do so until we see a change.

I, Zieland Anderson, NBA player, businessman, and trailblazing citizen can change the world for the better. And I will do just that! One day, one camp, and one life at a time!

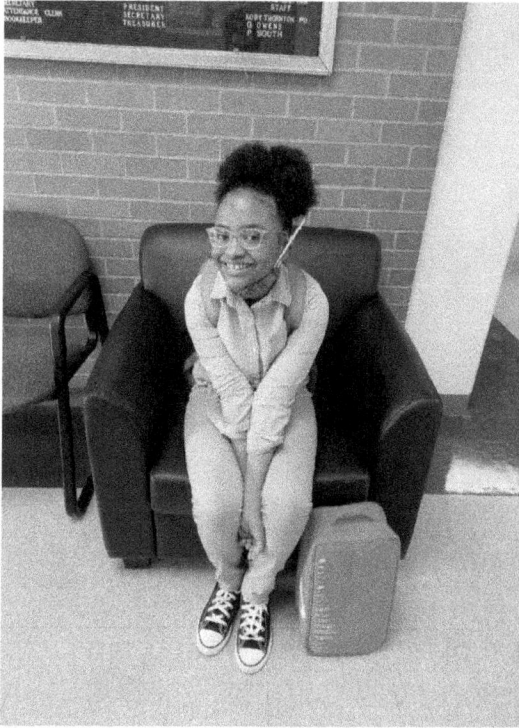

Ava Ramos

"The measure of intelligence is the ability to change."

Albert Einstein

I also want to dedicate my contribution to this book to my mom, my dad, my brother, and the rest of my family. I want to say thank you to my parents and my family. Without them, I would not be here. They always push me to be my best.

"Paging Dr. Ramos, You are needed to blaze your trail!"

Hello world! It is your friendly neighborhood fifth grader, and I am coming to share with you how I plan to make my mark and impact the world!

Even through an international pandemic, I have spent my final year in elementary school working hard to maintain straight A's! Let me tell you, it has not been easy, but my hard work is paying off! I am a very social person and I enjoy hanging out with my friends, so spending the last year and a half in quarantine has not exactly been peaches and cream.

I am from Louisville, Kentucky and I have lived there all my life. And if you know anything about Kentucky, you know that creating social activities are necessary if you want to have fun! Well unless of course you are into horses, then you will have plenty to keep you busy!

I enjoy my life and that includes a lot of what it brings my way. For example, art. I consider it a gift to my creative side. I love to draw, paint, and create things. It is so relaxing for me.

Now let me tell you, my greatest love of all is for my family! My parents, my little brother, my grandparents, and my cousins. It is funny how many of us have names that start with an "A" like Adam and

Ayan. I really enjoy spending time with all my cousins.

I have a great relationship with my mom and my dad. I am also very close to my little brother. He is very important to me and we enjoy spending time together and having fun!

As a big sister, it is really important to me that I set a good example for my little brother. Just as much as I want to be successful, I want the same thing for my little brother! The special bond that I share with my family members is what guides me to want to help other people to feel safe and loved in this world. I want to be an orthopedic surgeon when I grow up. I love helping people, so I think being a doctor is a great way to do that.

It all started in preschool; you know my love for art. I mean, what else does a 4-year-old do in school, but color and paint! I got my Crayola crayons and drew one line, and I was sold. That one line looked cool, so I kept on going and drew another. Well after about 10 more lines and crayon marks everywhere, I had completed my first masterpiece. That is when I realized that creating things with my hands made me feel more like a part of the worldwide community. I had things I could give to share some joy and help others. A huge fan of my "art" career is my grandmother on my dad's side of my

family (also known as "Granny").
Her support is a big part of my love
for the art life as well. Granny
allowed me to share my art with her
and even turn her apartment into
my own art gallery. She would tell
me to write my name and the date
on each piece and never failed to
hang up each one in her living room.
I cannot be sure how many drawings
I made, but I know it was a lot. And
Granny loved every one like it was
an original Van Gogh painting.

I am not only passionate about drawing in my life, but I am also passionate about helping others. And using my ability to change and grow is how I plan to become a helping doctor in the truest meaning of that idea. I want to be an orthopedic surgeon. An orthopedic surgeon is a doctor who specializes in the musculoskeletal system. For example, bones, muscles, ligaments, tendons, and joints are a part of this system. Being an orthopedic surgeon is very important because the musculoskeletal system is pretty much our whole body. To move and do the things we do in life, we need our bones, joints, and ligaments to work together. I believe the musculoskeletal system is a lot like the world. All the parts of the system are needed to make up the whole body. The whole body can grow and function because it is connected to everything it needs to do so. That is how our community grows in real life.

By each person connecting to the other and helping one another, the community grows stronger and more productive. Therefore, I love helping people and I think being a doctor is a great way to do that. It will take a lot of hard work and dedication, but I have no doubt I am up for the challenge. I will use my leadership skills and ability to help others through medicine to impact one of the most hurtful human illnesses in the world today: RACISM. The existence of racism is so unfair and unkind.

Judging someone's worth by the color of their skin is inhumane. We are all unique in our own way and that is what helps the world to be so successful. The talents of all of us joining together to compliment the others. Something great can come from joining together.

Racism uses the thing we cannot change to keep others oppressed. I say that personality is a better way to tell about who someone truly is inside. With issues like racism and world hunger, we should be more focused on helping one another instead of judging one another and being violent against each other. Seeing people beg for food on the sidewalks and seeing them hungry makes me sad.

Sickness and poor nutrition come from world hunger. Is that not more important than my skin color or your skin color? Poverty is overtaking the entire world. People are living on the streets and do not have enough money to care for themselves. People demean others, using hurtful words to frighten and control other people.

This impacts the mental mood of those who are verbally attacked causing depression, decreased self-esteem, PTSD, and mood changes.

All these things cause a huge problem in the world: oppression of the entire human race. And it should not matter what color we are, we should work together to solve these problems for everyone. From practicing medicine privately, I will make a lot of money to invest in helping others. My plan is to focus on fighting against racism to overcome the effects of it like violence and poverty, especially world hunger.

People who are suffering from diseases will be treated by my practice even if they do not have money or insurance and regardless of their skin tone. I will treat each person with respect and dignity. I will host fundraisers within my circle and network. The money will contribute to the organization of a shelter that will be established to support victims of oppression.

The shelter will be known as Ava's Safe Haven. I will use my earnings and fundraising money to start programs that support victims of racism, violence, poverty, and hunger.

People can donate to my foundation and the money can go to the people that are less fortunate. And in no time, I will be available to serve and help in any way I can.

Inside of Ava's Safe Haven, there will be an art studio used to host events for children to express themselves artistically.

It will be dedicated in honor of my grandmother and named "Granny's Art Gallery and Showcase Studio."

This studio and gallery setup will offer free professional art classes to those who have struggled with overcoming the effects of poverty, hunger, homelessness, violence, and racism and want to express it through art.

The gallery will showcase their work and people who come to the gallery can admire and purchase artwork.

The funds from the purchases will go directly to the artist to help them live a safer life.

This program will be open to all and free, so no one misses the opportunity due to a lack of money.

Anyone who needs help can come to the haven to receive it. Every race is always welcomed at the haven for love, support, and help. And in no time, I will be available to serve and help in any way I can.

I know that my world-class surgeon hands will be what makes it possible for me to help support victims of any kind of abuse.

And in no time, I will be available to serve and help in any way I can.

If anyone ever needs me, they can ask for the hospital to call out, Paging Dr. Ava!

Semaj Ellis

"Nothing in life that's worth anything is easy."
President Barack Obama

Hello, my name is Semaj Ellis, I am in 6th grade and I go to Western Middle School for the Arts. I am a 2020 graduate of Shacklette and am privileged to remain connected to my elementary school. As a student, I have always made good grades and high rankings on my tests. I have also participated in the Mayor's Cup. I plan to challenge myself by entering the Advanced Program in the coming school year.

My education is something I greatly value and it is something my family takes very seriously.

The thing that I enjoy the most about life is being a part of a multicultural world where I can learn about the differences between human beings. The differences that we celebrate and honor. With that said, the existence of white supremacy and hate crimes against Asian Americans, Arab Americans, and African Americans is growing in a negative way in our country. This is something that I would like to change about the world. I wish I could just erase all negativity from the Earth. The assumption that all people are the same way based on their ethnicity and heritage alone is just wrong and leads to pain, division, and violence in our world.

Racist and uninformed people think all African Americans are "thugs" or "gangbangers". People think every person of Arabic heritage is a "terrorist." They believe that every Asian person looks the same. These beliefs are just as wrong as someone who is not white believing that every white person is racist. It bothers me that people do not take the time to truly get to know someone but want to judge them and even keep them from succeeding in life. It shows how small-minded people can be. Of course, I am aware of the local and national happenings.

I just wish I could walk around my city knowing that no one is being treated disgustingly or unfairly. I also wish I could change poverty for everyone. There are so many kids in this world that must wonder or hope they will have a warm meal each night. I just wish no kid or adult had to go through this. All these things inspire me to work hard and be grateful for what I have that others lack. I am not worried about being cared for and having what I need.

Thanks to my parents, I have clothes to wear and never have to worry about having a warm meal. I cannot be selfish or ungrateful knowing some kids do not have half of the things I have.

What really got me interested in this subject is when George Floyd and Breonna Taylor were killed. It reminded me how bad the public and the police treat the African American community. I was also hearing about these Asian hate crimes around America. All these racist people need to put themselves into other people's shoes, then they will see how it feels to be harassed and be name called all because of race. I want to show people that all black people are not bad people. The things racist people do and say to us can shake our confidence, but we are some of the smartest people on this earth, who built the pyramids? People are so amazed by the pyramids they have gone so far to say aliens built it. They believe the Egyptians did not do it because they think African people are not smart enough to be architects.

On this Earth, African Americans are not valued and are widely oppressed. Even with the progress we have made, we still have a long way to go. I want to contribute to shortening that distance. To this day, we must fight for what we have. I want to be successful so I can speak out and people will listen. I feel like I can really change the world through words. I know I can.

I really know I can change the world because look at all the people that came before me. For example, Martin Luther King, Malcolm X, and Barack Obama. All these people who are known by many, did not start rich or famous, they worked for what they believed in and got the African American people involved. I am not rich or famous, but if I fight for what I believe in like them, I too, can make a difference. We cannot continue as if nothing is wrong.

If we can all join peacefully and fight for our community to become stronger, we will definitely see a change. People think that movements like Black Lives Matters are useless or do not matter, but they do. If we do not do anything, it is going to keep happening. Violence against minorities and the rise of police brutality is growing every day. Just because we do not acknowledge every case, does not mean it is not happening. Between the year 2014 and 2020, at least 7,680 African Americans were killed due to police brutality.

But people still say the problem does not exist. People still say there is no use in fighting back. This world may never be completely fair and just, but it will become better if we keep trying. I will never lose faith in that or this movement.

I feel like the trail I blaze will travel around the world creating opportunities for equality for African Americans, Asians, and other oppressed people. I also feel like it will thrive in the African American communities. I talked a lot about the Black Lives Matter movement because I am passionate about seeing the fair treatment and equal opportunity for my African

American brothers and sisters. I feel like it will really impact America and I hope it impacts the world. The world needs to understand that intentional negative behavior, racism, and violence will only make our world worse. I know justice, fairness, peacefulness, and equality are exactly what the world needs to heal the pain and become better. I am certain that my trail with make a path to better!

www.ingramcontent.com/pod-product-compliance
Lightning Source LLC
Chambersburg PA
CBHW052101270326
41931CB00012B/2850